FOOD & FEASTS

WITH THE

AZTECS

Imogen Dawson

New Discovery
B·O·O·K·S
Parsippany, New Jersey

First American publication 1995 by New Discovery Books, an imprint of Silver Burdett Press.
A Simon & Schuster Company
299 Jefferson Road, Parsippany, NJ 07054

First published in 1995 in Great Britain by
Wayland (Publishers) Ltd

A ZOË BOOK

Copyright © 1995 Zoë Books Limited

Devised and produced by
Zoë Books Limited
15 Worthy Lane
Winchester
Hampshire SO23 7AB
England

Printed in Italy by Grafedit SpA.
Design: Jan Sterling, Sterling Associates
Picture research: Victoria Sturgess
Maps and illustrations: Gecko Limited
Production: Grahame Griffiths

10 9 8 7 6 5 4 3 2 1

Silver Burdett 11-22 1/97

Library of Congress Cataloging-in-Publication Data

Dawson, Imogen.
    Food & feasts with the Aztecs / Imogen Dawson.
        p. cm. — (Food & feasts)
    Includes bibliographical references and index.
    ISBN 0-02-726318-5
    1. Aztecs—Food—Juvenile literature. 2. Food habits—
Mexico—History—Juvenile literature. 3. Aztec Cookery—
Juvenile literature. [1. Food habits—Mexico. 2. Aztecs—
Social life and customs. 3. Aztec cookery.] I. Title.
II. Title: Food and feasts with the Aztecs. III. Series.
F1219.76.F67D39 1994
394.1'2'0972—dc20   94-26599

Summary: A social history of life in the Aztec Empire just before the Spanish conquest, explaining why certain foods were eaten and describing how they were prepared or cooked. Includes information about events that brought about special celebrations and feasts.

Photographic acknowledgments

The publishers wish to acknowledge, with thanks, the following photographic sources:

Ancient Art & Architecture Collection 23t; B.T.Batsford Ltd 16t; Biblioteca Medicea Laurenziana, Florence 7t, 8c&br, 12tr, 13t, 16bl&r, 22c, 24b; Bibliothèque de l'Assemblée nationale, Paris 9b, 12tl; Bibliothèque Nationale, Paris 9t, 22t; The Bodleian Library, Oxford 3 (Ms.Arch.Selden A.1,fol.61r), 5 (Ms.Arch.Selden A.1, fol.46r), 7b (Ms.Arch.Selden A.1, fol.68r), 11&12b (Ms.Arch.Selden A.1, fol.60r), 13b (Ms.Arch.Selden A.1, fol.71r), 17b, 19 (Ms.Arch.Selden A.1, fol.2r), 23b (Ms.Arch.Selden A.1, fol.69r); The Bridgeman Art Library title page, 20r; Detenal, Mexico 10b; C.M.Dixon 21; The Fotomas Index 25; Peter Newark's Western Americana 18r; Richard Townsend 8bl; Werner Forman Archive 24t/British Museum, London 14t, 22b/Liverpool Museum 15t/Museum für Völkerkunde, Berlin 17t/National Museum of Anthropology, Mexico City 6t&b/St.Louis Art Museum, USA 14b.

Cover: Biblioteca Medicea Laurenziana, Florence top left & center; Bibliothèque de l'Assemblée nationale, Paris bottom left; The Bodleian Library, Oxford bottom right (Ms.Arch.Selden A.1, fol.60r); Werner Forman Archive/British Museum, London top right.

The publishers have made every effort to trace the copyright holders, but if they have inadvertently overlooked any, they will be pleased to make the necessary arrangement at the first opportunity.

CONTENTS

INTRODUCTION

Spanish explorers first reached the coast of Central America in the early 1500s. They had come from the Spanish **colony** on the island of Cuba, in the Caribbean. When they returned to Cuba, the explorers told stories about a rich and powerful kingdom, with huge amounts of gold, that was said to lie west of the mountains on the mainland.

Captain Hernán Cortés was ordered to find out if the stories were true. If so, he was to take control or conquer the kingdom and bring back the gold for the king of Spain. Cortés led 100 sailors and 400 soldiers on this expedition and reached the mainland coast in 1519. The kingdom that Cortés found beyond the mountains was the center of the Aztec **empire**, ruled by Montezuma II (1502–1520).

It had taken the Aztecs about 200 years to build up their empire in what is now central

▽ By 1519 the Aztec empire stretched from the desert in the north to the hills of Oaxaca in the south. The Aztecs also controlled a trade route leading south along the Pacific coast to Xoconochco. More than 15 million people lived in the lands controlled by the Aztecs.

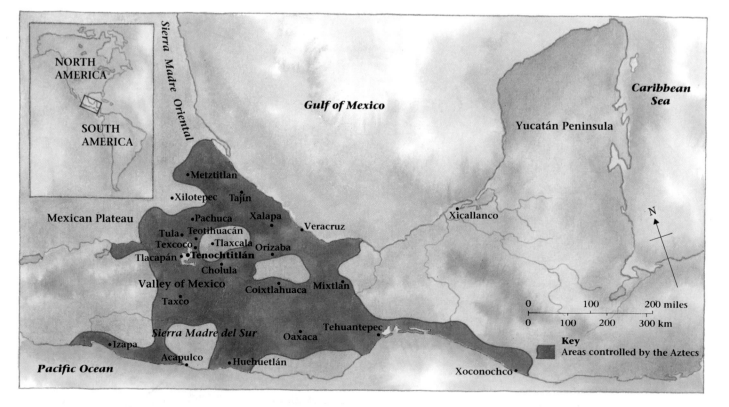

NORTH AMERICA

SOUTH AMERICA

Sierra Madre Oriental

Gulf of Mexico

Caribbean Sea

Yucatán Peninsula

Mexican Plateau

•Metztitlan

•Xilotepec Tajin

•Pachuca Xalapa

•Xicallanco

Tula• Teotihuacán

•Veracruz

Texcoco• •Tlaxcala Orizaba

Tlacapán• •**Tenochtitlán**

Cholula

Valley of Mexico

Coixtlahuaca Mixtlan

Taxco•

N

0   100   200 miles

0   100   200   300 km

Sierra Madre del Sur Oaxaca Tehuantepec

•Izapa

Key
Areas controlled by the Aztecs

Acapulco• •Huehuetlán

Pacific Ocean

Xoconochco•

The name Aztec comes from the word *Aztlán*, which means "place of the cranes" in the Nahuatl language. Most of the Aztec peoples spoke this language. In Aztec **legend**, Aztlán was the homeland of the Mexica people. The Mexica left Aztlán and moved south to settle in the Valley of Mexico. Peoples from other areas also settled there, but within 300 years, the Mexica had become the most powerful. By the time the Spanish arrived, all the people in the valley called themselves Mexica. Later, historians used the word *Aztec* to describe all the different peoples who lived in the Valley of Mexico at the time of the Spanish **conquest**.

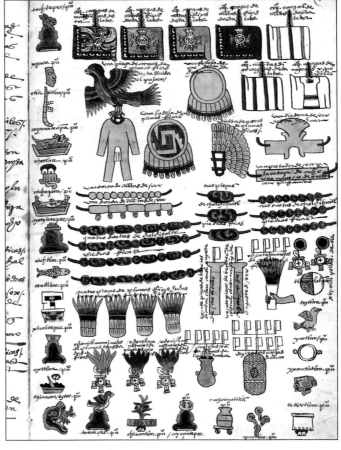

The Spaniards were amazed when they first saw the Valley of Mexico. Bernal Díaz, who served under Cortés, wrote this description in his book *The Conquest of New Spain*.

"And when we saw all those cities and villages built in the water, and other great towns on dry land . . . we were astounded. Indeed, some of our soldiers asked whether it was not all a dream."

Mexico. First they took control of the most **fertile** farmland in the Valley of Mexico. The Aztecs traded with peoples in different areas. As they became more powerful, the Aztecs forced people to pay **tribute** to them, not only in the countryside but also in many towns and **city-states**. The Aztecs were greatly feared and had made many enemies throughout their empire.

When Montezuma II became ruler in 1502, the Aztec empire was still growing. During his rule it stretched from the Atlantic to the Pacific coasts. It was controlled from the capital city, Tenochtitlán, in the Valley of Mexico.

About one million people lived in the valley when Cortés arrived there in November 1519. Villages, towns, and cities were built not only on land but also on islands and swampland in the lakes, where they were surrounded by water. More than a quarter of the people lived in Tenochtitlán itself. With a population of more than 250,000, the city was four times the size of London and far bigger than any city in Europe at that time.

△ Here is a page from Montezuma's records, showing the amounts of tribute due from some towns.

The Aztecs had a system of writing that used picture symbols, or glyphs, rather than letters of the alphabet.

The glyphs down the left side of the page are for the towns. The glyphs running across the page show the type of goods and the amount to be paid in tribute. These include warriors' uniforms, strings of jade beads, and containers filled with cacao (cocoa) beans.

The Aztecs had strict laws to control the peoples that they ruled and harsh punishments, including death, for those who disobeyed them. These laws covered the ownership of land, the payment of taxes, and the work people did. The Aztecs even controlled the clothes people could wear and what they were allowed to eat and drink.

The power of the gods and goddesses was greatly feared—more so than Aztec laws. People believed that they controlled everything that made life possible. The Aztecs' feasts, festivals, and patterns of everyday life were designed to ensure that the gods and goddesses would allow life on earth to continue.

Many temples to the gods were built on pyramid-shaped platforms throughout the empire. These temples were centers of religion and learning. Priests studied **astronomy**, surveying the stars and planets in the night sky, and produced an accurate yearly calendar. They used the calendar to set and record the dates for all the feasts and festivals to the gods. They also used their knowledge of the night skies as **astrologers**. They told people when to do important things, such as planting or harvesting crops.

Most of the crops the Aztecs grew were unknown in Europe at the time of the Spanish conquest. Tomatoes; avocados; chilies and peppers; potatoes; squash such as pumpkins; maize (corn); and tobacco were brought back to Europe by the Spanish. These crops have been grown in Europe ever since that time.

The Aztecs called the areas near the east coast on the Gulf of Mexico the "hot lands." Here **tropical** crops such as cacao,

△ This statue of Coatlicue, "Lady of the Serpent Skirt," once stood in the courtyard of the Great Temple at Tenochtitlán. The Aztecs believed she was the earth goddess, mother of the moon; the stars; and Huitzilopochtli, the warrior or sun god. He was believed to battle every night against darkness. As long as he won this battle, the sun rose every day.

Poor people drank water, but the favorite drink for rich Aztecs was *chocolatl*, chocolate. It was made by pounding cacao nuts and boiling them with maize flour. The mixture was strained, whipped to a stiff froth, and then served cold. Sometimes vanilla and spices were added to flavor this drink. Honey was often used to sweeten it. Sugar was unknown to the Aztecs.

▽ This drinking cup was used to hold *chocolatl*. It is in the shape of a hare. Only rich people could afford such beautiful cups.

◁ Most food was grilled, roasted, steamed, or boiled over an open fire.

The hearth, where three stones were arranged in a triangle to support the cooking pots and pans, was the center of every home. Chantico, the goddess of the house, was said to be in the fire that burned there, so it was kept lit all year round.

vanilla, rubber, cotton, pineapples, peanuts, and sweet potatoes were grown.

The Aztecs caught many kinds of fish from the rivers and lakes. Sometimes they hunted deer, rabbits, pigeons, and ducks. They also kept turkeys, ducks, and *itzcuintli*—small hairless dogs, which they fattened and ate on special occasions. Until the Spanish introduced cattle and sheep from Europe, the Aztecs had no dairy products, such as cheese and milk, and they ate very little meat.

Maize was the most important, or **staple**, food crop. Every part of the maize plant was used. The corn was ground to make flour for tortillas, a pancake-shaped bread, or boiled into a thin porridge called atole (*atolli* in Nahuatl). The leaves or husks were stuffed with fillings to make tamales, which were steamed over an open fire. The maize stalks were burned as fuel.

▽ This drawing from a codex page shows a feast of tamales and turkey.

Ordinary people held feasts when babies were born and when people died. They left offerings of quail, rabbits, tobacco, and flowers at the burial place every year at the Feast of the Dead.

Nobles held feasts more often. They gave gifts to their guests and handed out food to poor people.

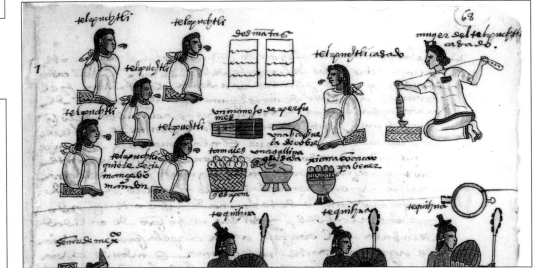

FARMING AND FOOD IN THE COUNTRYSIDE

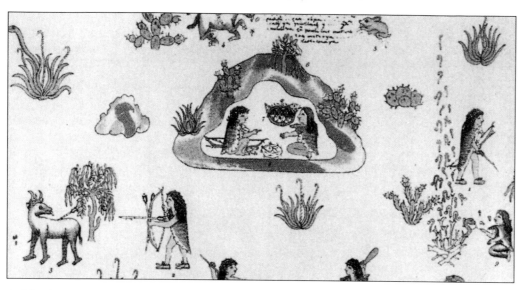

△ The Mexica came from the dry north. This illustration shows how they lived, by hunting and gathering food. They moved from place to place in search of food.

The Aztec farmers had no plows or carts or farm animals to pull them. They used digging sticks, which had long handles and wooden blades, to prepare the soil. These were easy to use in the light soil.

▷ The patterns of the Aztec farmers' terraces can still be seen on the hillsides today in Acolhuacan.

Most of the land in what was the Aztec empire is hilly and high. It is between 3,280 and 6,560 feet above sea level. In the north, the highlands get little rain, and the land is poor. People in these areas lived mainly by hunting animals and gathering wild plants.

Further south, the highlands get more rain. The soil is light but rich enough to grow crops. Here the Aztec farmers made flat strips of land, or terraces, on the hillsides to plant crops. There was always a danger of **drought**, if the rains failed to come.

▽ These pictures from a codex page show Aztec farmers using a digging stick to plant maize and then to hoe the weeds.

Mountain ranges separate the highlands from the east and west coasts. In the tropical "hot lands," on the east coast, there is plenty of rain all year round.

Here people cleared and burned the thick forest and undergrowth. Then they planted crops, particularly cacao. After two or three years, when the crops had taken most of the goodness out of the soil, the farmers moved on to clear a new area of land and plant crops.

The Valley of Mexico

The Valley of Mexico itself is more than 6,560 feet above sea level and is surrounded by mountains. High **altitudes** mean lower temperatures, so the climate is springlike for most of the year. In Aztec times, mountain streams fed the five shallow lakes in the valley. Much of the fertile farmland here was watered, or **irrigated**, from the freshwater streams. Different crops were planted throughout the year. The Aztecs **fertilized** their land to ensure that crops grew well.

During the dry winters the streams would sometimes dry up. If there was too little or too much rain in the summer, the crops might fail, and there would be a **famine**. Although three-quarters of the people living in the Valley of Mexico in Aztec times farmed the land, they could not produce enough food for all the people in the towns and cities there. One of the reasons that the Aztecs built up

▽ This drawing of Tlaloc, "he who makes things grow," comes from a codex made before the Spanish conquest.

The rain god's clothing and his face mask, shaped like goggles, are painted blue, the color of water. The white feathers on his headdress stand for white clouds, and the black on his body stands for storm clouds.

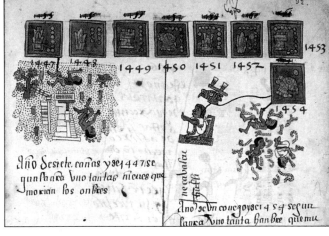

△ The Aztecs recorded the most important events in their history. This page from a codex shows people dying and dead from starvation. Four years of drought had led to a terrible famine in 1454. The fear of another famine was always on people's minds.

In spring, at the end of the dry season, farmers prayed and danced. They made sacrifices to the rain god Tlaloc to send rain so that the new crops would grow.

▷ The mud that was piled up to make the chinampas was held in place by posts and a **wicker** framework or fence. Willow trees were planted at each corner. Their roots also helped to keep the mud in place.

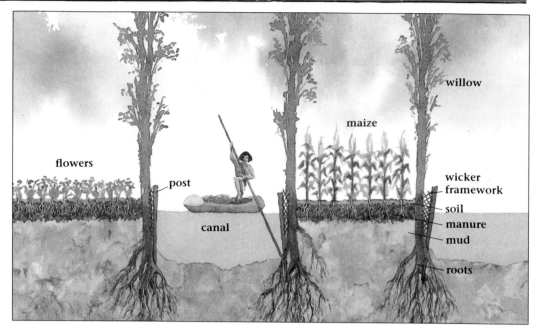

flowers

post

canal

maize

willow

wicker framework

soil

manure

mud

roots

Farmers could grow and harvest as many as seven crops a year on their chinampas. To keep the soil fertile, they spread fresh mud from the lake onto their land and dug in animal waste.

their empire was to bring in supplies of food from other areas.

The Aztecs farmed every available piece of land in the Valley of Mexico. They dug out water channels, or canals, through the marshes around the lakes. Plants and small bushes were cut down and piled up with mud from the canals. They made rectangular platforms of land called chinampas. Some of these island plots were very small, about 5 feet wide and 50 feet long, but most were about 300 feet long and between 15 feet and 30 feet wide.

Farmers and their families lived on the larger chinampas. Their small houses had mud walls and the roofs were **thatched** with reeds.

Most farmers kept a few black bees (which had no sting) for honey and wax. They made beehives from sections of hollowed-out tree trunks, which were then sealed with mud at each end.

◁ The pattern of the chinampas and the network of canals between them can still be seen in this aerial photograph of the Valley of Mexico.

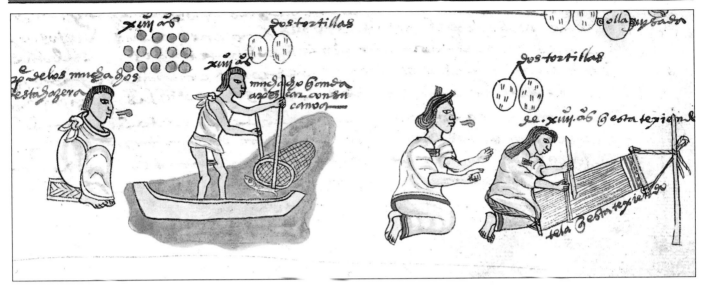

△ These drawings, from a codex made just after the Spanish conquest, show parents teaching their children. The boy on the left is learning to fish; the girl on the right is learning to weave cloth.

The ovals above their heads show the number of tortillas they were allowed to eat.

The farmers kept turkeys in mud huts near their houses. They fed their turkeys, ducks, and dogs with corn, bread, and other food scraps.

Farmers grew vegetables such as tomatoes, chilies, onions, squash, and many different kinds of beans on the chinampas. They also grew fruit, flowers, and **herbs** such as cilantro and sage. They took the fresh produce to the markets in the towns and cities by boat, along the network of waterways between the chinampas.

Farming families started work at dawn. The men and the boys worked on the land, went fishing, or brought back firewood by canoe. The girls and the women spent most of their time at home, preparing food, weaving cloth, and looking after the animals.

Families ate their first meal of the day together at about 10 A.M. This was often a bowl of porridge, made from grains such as maize, amaranth, or chia, the seeds from a kind of sage plant.

Everyone, rich or poor, ate the main meal during the hottest part of the day. For most families the meal was a simple one—tortillas and beans, usually served with a spicy sauce made from chilies and tomatoes. Tamales, fish, and meat were eaten only on special occasions.

The last meal of the day was a bowl of thin porridge, or gruel, eaten at bedtime.

Aztec boats were canoes, made from hollowed-out tree trunks. It was easier to carry goods and people around the valley by water than on land. Canoes were also used for fishing and hunting around the lakes.

The Aztecs had no other form of transportation. They carried goods on their backs when they were traveling over land.

Tortillas were made fresh every day, as they became dry and inedible after a few hours. They were cooked over the fire on a flat clay plate called a comal.

Chia was also crushed to make oil that was used in paints and varnishes.

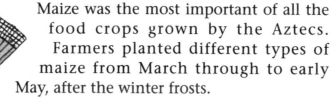

The most important crops

Maize was the most important of all the food crops grown by the Aztecs. Farmers planted different types of maize from March through to early May, after the winter frosts.

The maize seeds were planted next to squash plants. When the young maize plants started to grow, the big broad leaves of the squash shaded the maize from the hot sun. The shade also helped to keep the soil moist, until the heavy rains came in July and August.

By mid-July each maize plant had two or three young corncobs. Some of these were picked and used to make maize cakes, but one cob was left growing on each plant.

In September, when the corn was yellow and ripe, it was harvested. The best corn seed was saved, ready to plant the following spring. The rest of the maize was shelled and stored in clay pots or large wickerwork bins until it was needed for cooking.

Amaranth was also an important crop for the Aztecs. It ripened before the maize crop, so was harvested earlier. If the maize crop failed, people still had amaranth seeds with which to make porridge and flour. Women used amaranth dough to make small figures of the gods and goddesses, which were eaten during harvest festivals.

△ Here farmers are taking the young cobs of corn from the maize plants. The man on the right is bending back the corn leaves. The last cob left on the plant will now ripen and dry in the sun.

△ This picture, from a codex drawn before the Spanish conquest, shows a basket of corn.
A festival called Huey Tozoztli was held when the corn seed was due to be planted. Priests offered some of the corn to the gods and goddesses so that they would help the seeds to grow well.

It took a woman about six hours to make flour from ripe maize. First the corn was soaked overnight in lime-water to soften it. Then it was boiled and skinned. Finally, the corn was crushed by hand on a stone slab called a metate, with a stone roller, to make flour.

▽ Children between the ages of 11 and 14 were taught by their parents. These drawings show boys bringing back firewood and girls making tortillas.

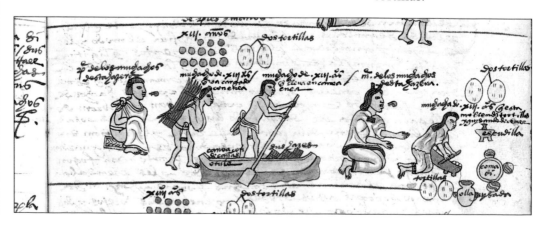

◁ These pictures show amaranth plants being harvested. The seeds are shaken from the plants and dried in the sun on reed mats. Then they are stored in clay pots.

A very special plant

The maguey cactus grows wild, but it was also planted by the Aztecs in dry areas. It does not need much water and is not killed by frost. Almost every part of the plant was used.

The spines of the cactus were made into sewing needles. The threads, or **fibers**, from the plant were woven to make coarse cloth. The thread was strong enough to make nets, bags, and even sandals. The leaves were dried and used to thatch roofs or were burned for fuel.

When the cactus flower was cut, juice or sap oozed out of the stem. One plant could provide more than five quarts of sap every day. The Aztecs collected the sap and stored it in skins or in dippers made from squash plants. They used the sap to make syrup for medicines and to make an alcoholic drink called *octli*. (The Spaniards called this pulque.)

Aztec treatments recorded by a Spanish priest, Fray Bernardino de Sahagún, just after the Spanish conquest.

For sore throats . . .
"Bee honey is to be drunk, and many times, by way of the nose, bee honey or thickened maguey syrup will drop into the throat."

For a cough . . .
"He is to drink boiled chili water, or atole (*atolli*) with yellow chili and honey. He will not drink cold water. He will abstain from chocolate, fruit and yellow maguey wine. He will avoid the cold, the chill . . . he will cover himself well."

▽ This drawing shows an old woman being served *octli* by her grandchildren

Aztec drinking laws were strict. People under 30 were not allowed to drink alcohol at all. People of 30 and over were allowed to drink two glasses of alcohol at festivals.

The only people who could drink alcohol every day were the very old—the Aztecs said their blood was "turning cold."

Aztec calendars

The priests used two different calendars to work out exactly when farmers should plant or harvest their crops and when there would be festivals and offerings to the gods.

One calendar was based, like ours, on a 365-day year, but there were only 52 years in an Aztec "century." Each year was given a name and number. The Aztecs divided their year into 18 months. Each month lasted 20 days. The five days left over at the end of each year were called "hollow" days. They were thought to be unlucky and dangerous, so people stayed at home and did very little during this time.

The Aztecs gave the months names that were linked to the seasons and patterns of farming. Month 1 was called "stopping of the water"; month 10, "fall of the fruits"; and month 16, "fall of the waters."

Most months had farming festivals. During month 4 (mid-April to mid-May) the festival of Huey Tozoztli, "the great awakening," was held in honor of many gods and goddesses, including Tlaloc, Chalchiuhtlicue, and Quetzalcoatl. Corn seed was blessed at this time.

△ This is an Aztec sculpture of the goddess of water, rivers, and lakes. Her name, Chalchiuhtlicue, means "she of the jade skirt." The Aztecs thought that the lakes looked the same color green as jade.

In month 8 (July), the festival of Huey Tecuilhuitl, "great feast of the lords," was held in honor of the young maize goddess Xilonen. Poor people were invited to feast with the rich and the ruler gave gifts to the poor.

▽ Quetzalcoatl, "feathered serpent" and lord of the winds, was shown in many different forms, often as a snake or a bird, or both, as his name suggests. Here he is shown as an Aztec porter, carrying a load of maize. People offered Quetzalcoatl gifts of incense, flowers, and birds.

The powers of the gods

The Spanish priests wanted the Aztec people to change their beliefs and become Christians. This was how Aztec priests explained the importance of their gods.

"They give us our daily fare and all that we drink, all that we eat, our food, maize, beans, amaranth, chia. We humbly ask them for water, for rain, with which everything flourishes on earth."

The priests used a second calendar to work out the best days and times for people to do

Some numbers, such as 3 and 7, were thought to be lucky, while others, such as 5 and 9, were thought to bring bad luck. However, days with these numbers were not always good or bad. The power of the gods on the day could change people's luck!

◁ A page from a codex that records Aztec religious ceremonies. The dots in the border are the 260 days in the year. In the center is the god of fire, Xiuhtecuhtli.

important things. It was based on the powers of the gods at particular times. This calendar was called the tonalpohualli, "the counting of the days." Each year was divided into 260 days. The days were grouped into 20 "weeks" of 13 days each.

The Aztecs believed that some gods were more powerful than others at certain times. For example, Quetzalcoatl, the wind god, was the most powerful god during the week of the wind, while Chalchiuhtlicue was the most powerful goddess during the week of the reed.

▽ These diagrams are drawn like cogs in a wheel, to show the way in which the 20-week cycle and the 13 days within each week were counted by the Aztecs and linked together.

Each week was given a name, such as dog, monkey, grass, or reed. The days within each week were numbered from 1 to 13. Therefore, each day of the year had a name and a number— 1 dog to 13 dog was followed by 1 monkey to 13 monkey and so on.

Tamales were a favorite food at Aztec feasts. The Spanish priest Sahagún describes some of the different ways in which they were prepared: "White tamales with beans forming a sea shell on top; tamales made of maize flowers with ground amaranth seeds and cherries added . . . tamales made with honey."

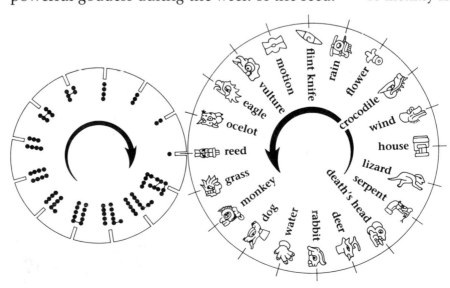

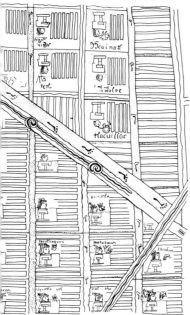

△ This map, drawn in the 16th century, shows part of the chinampa area around Tenochtitlán. The name of the family holding each plot of land is written in Aztec glyphs and in Spanish. The important canals are shown as wavy lines or curls. Footprints show where streets run alongside the canals.

Landholders and workers

Most farming families were part of a group, or calpulli. The calpulli owned and controlled lands in a particular area or neighborhood. Some land was farmed by everyone in the calpulli. The produce and income, or **revenue**, from it was used to maintain the local schools and temples, to provide food and medicines for the poor, and to entertain visitors to the neighborhood.

Each family also farmed its own land. The farm was passed on from parents to children, or **inherited**. If the land was not farmed well, the calpulli could take it away from the family, and hold it in "reserve." Then if another family needed more land, the calpulli might give them land from the reserve.

Free men and women peasants and workers were called *macehualtin*. If they left the neighborhood where they were born, they were no longer part of the calpulli, and had no claim to the land.

A large amount of farmland was owned by the *tlatoani*, the ruler. He gave some areas of land, or **estates**, to nobles, warriors, and officials. Their families could inherit the land, but the *tlatoani* could take the estates back if he so wished.

All Aztec boys were trained to fight, whether they were *macehualtin* or *pipiltin*. In times of war each calpulli was called on to supply warriors, weapons, food, and other supplies for the army. A *macehualli* who did well in battle might become an important warrior and a member of the *pipiltin*.

▽ The roots of this plant, *Iztac palancapatli*, were ground and made into a tea or powder. They were used to heal head wounds.

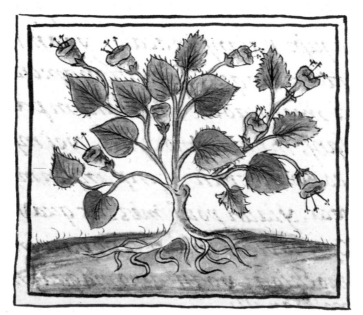

Aztec healers used about 1,200 plants for their medicines. Scientists have tested many of these plants and have shown that they were useful in treating the illnesses that the Aztecs described.

◁ *Quachtlacalhuaztli* was a herb used mainly to treat indigestion.

The ruling class was called the *pipiltin*. The peasants who worked the land for the *pipiltin* were called *mayeques*. They had no land of their own and were not allowed to leave the estates where they worked. They did not have the protection or help in times of need that was given to the *macehualtin* by the calpulli.

Weddings

Marriage was the start of adult life for the *macehualtin*. They were not full members of the calpulli until they married. Then the scribes listed them in the records as householders, and they had the right to farm a plot of land within the calpulli.

A wedding was a time for a great celebration, with music, dancing, and feasting that could last for four days. Many people were invited, from relatives and friends to the local school-teacher and important members of the calpulli.

After the marriage ceremony, the bride-groom's mother fed the bride and then the bridegroom with four mouthfuls of tamales, cooked in a special sauce. The guests could then start feasting.

Here the Spanish priest Sahagún describes the preparations for a wedding.
"Ground cacao was prepared, flowers were brought, tubes of tobacco were made up, sauce bowls and pottery cups and baskets were bought. Then maize was ground. . . . Tamales were made . . . perhaps for three days women made tamales."

△ Every Aztec family owned clay pots. Large ones were used for storing water, soaking maize, and cooking beans. Some families also owned mugs, plates, ladles, and bowls.
These are special bowls called *cajete*. The clay at the bottom of the bowls has been roughened with a crisscross pattern. *Cajete* were used to grate chili peppers.

▷ The picture at the top of this codex page shows a marriage ceremony. The man and woman on a reed mat have their clothes knotted together. This made them husband and wife.
At the bottom of the page you can see the food laid out for the wedding feast—a basket of tamales, turkey stew, and a big pot of *octli*.

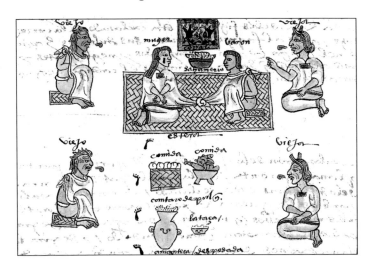

Some Aztec sayings

If a girl ate her meal standing up, she would marry a long way from home.

A woman who ate a tamale that had stuck to the side of the cooking pot would be unable to have children.

FOOD IN THE TOWNS AND CITIES

Every town was divided into neighborhoods, controlled by different groups, or *calpoltin*. The *macehualtin* who were born into these *calpoltin* often had a particular craft, trade, or skill, such as making pottery, baskets, or jewelry; weaving and dyeing cloth; or making tools or weapons.

People in the towns relied on the farmers to bring in supplies of food. The food was sold in the marketplace, which was near the main temple in most towns. Most of the food was bought fresh every day from the markets. The main way in which the Aztecs **preserved** food —kept it from going bad—was by drying or salting it.

Towns were the centers for collecting and recording the tribute from the surrounding areas. Much of the tribute was food, such as maize,

△ This map shows the towns and cities in the Valley of Mexico, at the time of the Spanish conquest. The 10-mile-long barrier was built by the Aztec poet-ruler Nezahualcoyotl. It kept the saltier lake water away from the fresher lake water around Tenochtitlán.

▷ This drawing of Tenochtitlán, which the Spanish called Mexico, was made in about 1576, more than 50 years after the Spanish conquest. The Spanish did not change the layout of the city, but they destroyed all the Aztec temples. They built churches on these sites instead.

Salty earth was collected from around the lakes during the dry season. First the earth was washed. The salty water, or brine, was heated in pottery jars. Then, as the water boiled off, brownish salt crystals were left at the bottom of the jars.

Salt crystals were sometimes stored in pots, but usually they were pressed into solid balls, blocks, or round cakes about the size of a loaf of bread.

which was kept in large storehouses. When the maize crop failed, Aztec officials distributed food from the storehouses to the local people.

Some officials traveled from town to town, checking the tribute before most of it was sent to the rulers in Tenochtitlán.

The growth of Tenochtitlán

When the Mexica arrived in the Valley of Mexico, they survived by hunting and fishing in the marshlands on the lakeshores. In the early 1300s they settled on a small rocky island on Texcoco, one of the five lakes in the valley.

Chinampas were made around the island as the settlement grew bigger. By the time the Spanish arrived, the city covered an area of about 20 square miles.

Most people used the canals between the chinampas to travel around the city. Supplies of food, firewood, and other heavy goods were brought to the city by boat. There were three main raised roads, or **causeways**, that linked the island city to the mainland.

Fresh drinking water for Tenochtitlán came from springs on the mainland. It was brought into the city by two raised channels, or **aqueducts**, from the south and the west. In some places the aqueducts opened out to become **reservoirs**. Here watersellers loaded the water into canoes and took it into the city.

A description by Bernal Díaz of Tenochtitlán, from *The Conquest of New Spain*.

"We saw a great number of canoes, some coming with food and others returning with goods for sale. . . . We saw that one could not pass from one house to another except over wooden bridges or by canoe. . . . We saw shrines that looked like gleaming white towers and castles: a marvelous sight. All the houses had flat roofs, and on the causeways were other small towers and shrines built like fortresses."

▷ In Aztec legend the Mexica were told to settle in the place where they saw an eagle nesting on top of a cactus plant. This was on the island in Lake Texcoco. The name, Tenochtitlán, means "cactus rock." The codex shows the founding of the city, with the eagle and cactus at the center of a blue cross, symbolizing Lake Texcoco.

The markets

The Aztec markets were busy and crowded. They were also friendly places, according to the Spanish priests who were in Mexico shortly after the Spanish conquest. People went to market not only to buy and sell goods, but also to meet friends and to hear the latest news.

The markets were well laid out, with different types of goods sold in particular areas. There were officials in every market to make sure that the produce was of good quality and that no one was cheated. They also fixed the prices for different goods.

An Aztec law made people bring their goods to sell in the markets, which were in all the towns. No one was allowed to sell anything on the way to the market.

◁ This artwork shows the types of goods and the prices that were fixed for **bartering** in Aztec markets.

▽ The detail from this modern painting, *The Market at Tenochtitlán*, by the famous Mexican artist Diego Rivera, shows what part of the market may have looked like in Aztec times.

20 lumps of rubber
= 1 cloak

string of jade beads
= 600 cloaks

100 cacao beans
= 1 cloak

feather cape
=100 cloaks

1 cloak

warrior costume
including headdress
and shield
= 64 cloaks

1 dugout canoe
= 1 cloak

100 sheets of paper
= 1 cloak

Coins were not used to buy goods. Instead, the Aztecs used cacao beans. People also exchanged, or bartered, using other goods such as feathers or ax blades. Everything in the market was sold by quantity or by a measure of length or capacity, never by weight. Maize and other food grains were sold in bins of different sizes. Length was measured by handspans, the distance a man could span with his arms outstretched, or the distance from the ground to a fingertip of a man's hand held high above his head.

The biggest market was in Tenochtitlán. About 25,000 people went there every day. There was a special market every fifth day, which attracted at least 40,000 people. The Spanish were amazed by its size and by the variety of goods for sale, as the description by Bernal Díaz shows.

▷ This little model is of the hairless dog that the Aztecs ate on special occasions.

"We went back to the great marketplace called Tlatelolco, and the swarm of people buying and selling. . . . Some of our soldiers who had been in Constantinople, in Rome and all over Italy, said that they had never seen such a market so well laid out, so large, so orderly and so full of people. . . .

There were chocolate merchants with their chocolate. . . . Sellers of kidney beans, sage and other vegetables and herbs, turkeys, rabbits, hares, deer, young ducks, little dogs and other such creatures. Then there were the fruiterers and the women who sold cooked food, flour and honey cake, and tripe. Each had their own part of the market. Then came pottery of all kinds, from big water jars to little jugs, after that there were those who sold honey . . . and other sweets like nougat . . . timber, beams and benches . . . sellers of firewood. . . .

I am forgetting the sellers of salt . . . and the fisherwomen and the men who sell small cakes. . . .

I wish I could tell of all the things which are sold there, but one would not have been able to see everything even in two days."

Bernal Díaz, *The Conquest of New Spain*

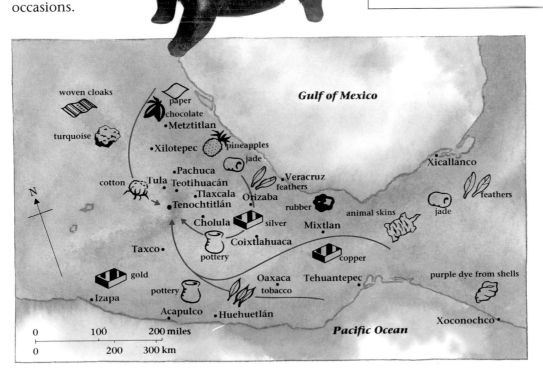

Gulf of Mexico

woven cloaks
paper
chocolate
• Metztitlan
turquoise
• Xilotepec — pineapples
jade
• Pachuca
cotton — Tula — Teotihuacán
• Veracruz
feathers
• Tlaxcala — Orizaba
• Tenochtitlán
rubber
• Cholula — silver
Mixtlan
animal skins
jade
Taxco •
Coixtlahuaca
pottery
copper
N
gold
Oaxaca
Tehuantepec
purple dye from shells
• Izapa
pottery
tobacco
Acapulco
• Huehuetlán
Xoconochco •
Xicallanco
feathers

0   100   200 miles
0   200   300 km

Pacific Ocean

◁ Many of the goods on sale at Tlatelolco came from distant parts of the Aztec empire, as this map shows.

A life of luxury

It was easy to see which people were nobles in any Aztec town. The *pipiltin* were the only people who were allowed to dress in fine cotton clothes and to wear expensive jewelry. The *pipiltin* paid no taxes and lived a life of luxury, enjoying feasts, music, games, and gambling. However, they could be called into battle as warriors by the *tlatloani* at any time.

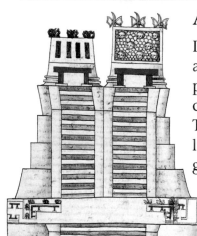

△ This drawing from a codex shows the main temple to the gods at Tenochtitlán. It was built on a platform or pyramid, like a mountain, which was a symbol of life for the Aztecs. The skull rack on the right shows that human sacrifices were made to the gods, to ensure that life on earth would continue.

"The noble here has some new houses which are as good as the best in Spain. They are large and well built. . . . There are both upper and lower rooms and very refreshing gardens with many trees and sweet-scented flowers . . . and bathing places of fresh water. . . . The noble has a large orchard near his house. . . . Within it is a great square pool of fresh water. . . . The pool contains many fish and different kinds of ducks."

From a letter Hernán Cortés sent to King Charles V of Spain

Hunting

Nobles had no need to hunt for food. They hunted birds such as quail and pigeon for fun, using blowpipes that fired small pellets. Ordinary people, using traps and nets, hunted deer and rabbits. The skins were used to make clothes for the *pipiltin*. In the "hot lands" people hunted **ocelots**. These skins were used to make warriors' costumes and cloaks for the Aztec nobles.

Each Aztec town provided an army of its own. The smallest unit was 20 soldiers. These units were combined into larger groups of 200, 400, or 800 warriors, commanded by *pipiltin* officers. The *tlatloani* was the commander in chief and often led the army into battle.

Between the ages of 15 and 20, noble boys went to the calmecac, or temple school, and were taught only by priests. They learned religion and history. The rules were strict. Boys had to take cold baths every day.

△ This drawing from a codex shows herbs being gathered in a **botanical** garden.

The *tlatloani* collected plants and trees from all over the empire. He grew them in botanical gardens in the Valley of Mexico. They were used for food and medicines.

◁ Only nobles and priests were allowed (and could afford) to buy this type of pottery. It came from the town of Cholula. The eating bowl is decorated with Aztec symbols. The two cups were for drinks such as *octli*.

The ruler

The *tlatloani*, "he who speaks," was the ruler of the Aztec empire. He controlled the priests, the *pipiltin*, and the army. The *tlatloani* lived in a palace close to the main temple at Tenochtitlán. He was treated like a living god.

The *tlatloani* was chosen, or **elected**, as ruler by a small number of *pipiltin*, including his own relatives, leading warriors, and priests. He was expected to wage war as often as possible. This would increase the amount of tribute and land for the Aztecs.

War would also provide prisoners to be sacrificed to the gods. There would be plenty of food for feasts, and the nobles could give gifts to their friends and the poor.

"For each meal his servants prepared more than thirty dishes . . . which they put over small earthenware braziers to prevent them from getting cold. They cooked more than three hundred plates of the food the ruler was going to eat and more than a thousand more for his guards. Every day they cooked turkeys, pheasants, duck, venison, pigeons, hares, and rabbits. . . . Then they brought him maize cakes and bread.

When he began his meal they placed a screen in front of him, so that no one should see him eat. His food was served on Cholula ware, some red and some black. . . . His servants brought him some of every kind of fruit that grew in the country, but he ate very little of it. Sometimes they brought him chocolate in cups of pure gold.

When he had finished his dinner and the singing and dancing were over, he would smoke from tubes, which were painted and filled with some herbs called tobacco. He took very little of it, and then fell asleep."

A description of Montezuma II, from Bernal Díaz, *The Conquest of New Spain*

△ This dagger was used for human sacrifice by the Eagle Warriors. Only nobles could belong to this unit of warriors.

When they captured enemy soldiers in battle, the warriors brought them to the temple at Tenochtitlán. The prisoners' hearts were sacrificed to the gods, and their heads were displayed on the skull rack.

The remains of the bodies were given to the relatives of the warriors who had captured them. The pieces were cooked in a stew with chilies and tomatoes. They were eaten at a feast to celebrate the victory and to make sure that the enemy's strength passed into the Aztecs.

▷ This page from a codex shows the last ruler of the Aztecs, Montezuma II, in his palace at Tenochtitlán.

FOOD FOR TRAVELERS

△ Very little remains today of the Aztec waterways around Tenochtitlán. This photograph of the chinampas was taken in an area south of Mexico City.

There were resthouses, shelters, and even public lavatories along the roads. All the roads and bridges were kept in good repair.

In some places canoes ferried people and goods across the rivers.

In the Valley of Mexico most people traveled by canoe. Some large canoes could take up to 60 passengers or a 3-ton cargo such as maize. The Aztecs built paved roads in their towns and cities, but in the countryside the roads were dirt tracks. Maize, beans, and squash were planted along the roadside and near ponds and lakes so that people in need of food could take it. The punishment for stealing a farmer's crops was death!

The roads were busy for most of the year, but particularly at harvest time. Teams of porters carried foodstuffs to the storehouses in the towns as tribute. Each porter carried a load of about 48 pounds and covered about 15 miles in a day.

Relays of runners, who carried letters and small packages for the *pipiltin*, could cover 148 miles in one day. This was how oysters, crabs, fresh fish, and pineapples were brought from the "hot lands" on the coast to Tenochtitlán, for the nobles' feasts.

Food for the army

There might be as many as 200,000 people to feed when the Aztecs went to war. As the army marched to battle, each town along the way had to provide food and lodging for the soldiers. Tribute towns had to send supplies of food—maize cakes, maize meal, toasted maize, beans, chilies, pumpkin seeds, and salt. Soldiers carried extra food in their backpacks. Taking food from the farmers or destroying their crops was strictly forbidden.

Before the *tlatloani* decided to wage war, he talked to the *pochteca*, who were long-distance traders and **merchants**. They were also spies,

The Aztecs used wheels on children's pull-along toys, but they did not build carts to transport goods because they had no pack animals to pull the carts.

▽ The only way people could carry freight on the narrow tracks over the hills and mountains was in backpacks.

The pack had a wooden frame—two upright poles with crosspieces. A rope, or tumpline, went around the wearer's head and to the bottom of the pack frame. It helped to take the weight of the load.

▷ Cortés and his soldiers followed the same route as the *pochteca* from the coast, over the mountains and into the Valley of Mexico.

As they traveled, the people gave them "maize cakes, fish, and fruit," according to Bernal Díaz.

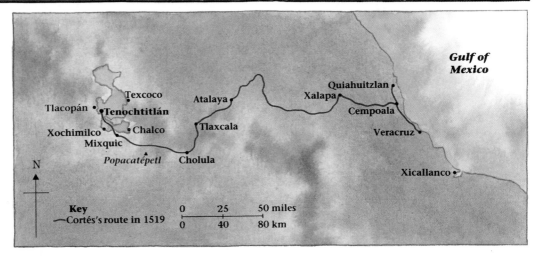

Gulf of Mexico

Quiahuitzlan
Xalapa
Cempoala
Texcoco
Atalaya
Tlacopán
Tenochtitlán
Veracruz
Xochimilco Chalco
Tlaxcala
Mixquic
Popacatépetl Cholula
Xicallanco

N

Key
— Cortés's route in 1519

| 0 | 25 | 50 miles |
| 0 | 40 | 80 km |

reporting on the wealth of the lands they visited outside the Aztec empire.

Pochteca were born into a calpulli. Although they were often wealthier than the *pipiltin*, they dressed very simply and lived a very secret life. They slipped out of Tenochtitlán at night, with canoe loads of trading goods—gold ornaments, rabbit fur, herbs for medicines, clothing, and pottery. They had large teams of armed porters to guard against robbers. The *pochteca* had resthouses and storehouses in cities throughout the empire.

It was the *pochteca* who first sent news to the *tlatloani* of the Spanish landing on the coast. They also reported on the progress of the Spanish expedition as it marched toward Tenochtitlán.

Before the *pochteca* set out on a long journey, they held a feast. Older merchants made speeches to warn of the dangers of rough roads, deserts, and swollen rivers. They also listed the discomforts of the journey—unseasoned food, stale tortillas, soggy maize, and foul water.

The Spaniards destroyed Tenochtitlán and conquered the Aztec empire. Montezuma and many thousands of Aztecs were killed in the fighting. Others died later from diseases that came from Europe. Very few Aztecs survived, and, under Spanish rule, their way of life was gone forever.

◁ This drawing from a codex shows Cortés meeting Montezuma II. The deer, quail, and maize at the bottom of the picture show the supplies of food that the Aztecs gave to Cortés for his soldiers.

MEALS AND RECIPES

Corn, tomatoes, potatoes, peppers, turkeys, pineapples, peanuts, and chocolate are some of the foods the Aztecs ate but that were unknown in Europe at the time of the Spanish conquest.

Today these foods are enjoyed all over the world. Trucks, trains, and planes can quickly transport fresh fruits such as pineapples from the tropics to other parts of the world. Many foods such as corn and other vegetables can be canned or frozen to preserve them.

The Spanish not only brought Aztec foods to Europe—the Old World—but also introduced animals such as cattle and sheep to the lands they conquered in the New World. Many of the popular dishes and snacks eaten in Mexico today combine Spanish and Aztec ingredients and styles of cooking.

The recipes here are for dishes that the Aztecs may have eaten. These dishes do not contain meat or dairy products from the animals that the Spanish introduced from Europe.

Food that is preserved by drying or salting tastes different from canned or frozen food. The Aztec meals you make will not taste exactly the same as the ones served by the Aztecs to the Spanish soldiers when they arrived in Tenochtitlán.

> **WARNING:** Sharp knives and boiling liquids are dangerous. Hot ovens and pans can burn you. *Always ask an adult to help you* when you are preparing or cooking food in the kitchen.

The Aztecs called the sauces they made mole. Their word for avocado is aguacate. The Mexicans call this avocado sauce guacamole. Sometimes it is served with a main meal, but people often serve it as a dip with tortilla chips.

Avocado dip

Ingredients

3 large ripe avocados

2 limes

1 onion

$^1/_2$ tsp chili powder

salt

1 T freshly chopped cilantro

2 tomatoes

2 bags of tortilla chips

1. Wash and dry the avocados. With a sharp knife, carefully make a cut around them, down to the pit in the middle of each fruit. Be sure to keep your fingers away from the knife blade.
2. Separate the two avocado halves and remove the pit with a spoon. Using your fingers or a knife, peel off the outside skin.
3. Chop up the flesh into small pieces and put it into the mixing bowl. Mash it with a fork until it is smooth.
4. Cut the fresh limes in half. Take out the seeds. Squeeze the lime juice into the mashed avocado and stir it in.
5. Carefully peel and chop the onion very fine with a sharp knife. Be sure to keep your fingers away from the knife blade. Add the onion and the chili powder to the mixture.
6. Stir the mixture well. Add salt to taste. Spoon the mixture into serving bowls.
7. Rinse the fresh cilantro leaves and dry them. Chop them fine and sprinkle them over the avocado dip to decorate it.
8. Wash and dry the tomatoes. Then cut them into quarters and serve them separately, with the tortilla chips.

Equipment

sharp knife

chopping board

spoon

mixing bowl

fork

lemon squeezer

serving bowls

Ask an adult to help you when you start to cook.

Sharp knives are dangerous.

Corn or bean soup

Ingredients

1 cup canned corn *or* canned kidney beans

1 large onion

3 tomatoes

1 tsp chili powder

salt

1 T freshly chopped cilantro

Ask an adult to help you when you start to cook.

You can make this soup with corn *or* with kidney beans, whichever you prefer.

1. Drain the canned beans *or* corn. Then measure them. Put the beans *or* corn in a large saucepan and cover them with water.
2. Carefully peel and chop the onion very fine, using a sharp knife. Be sure to keep your fingers away from the knife blade.
3. Wash the tomatoes and peel off the skins. Chop the tomatoes coarsely with a knife.
4. Add the chopped tomatoes, onion, and the chili powder to the saucepan and stir everything together.
5. Bring the mixture in the saucepan to a boil and then simmer it gently for 15 minutes.

Equipment

colander

measuring cup

large saucepan

chopping board

sharp knife

potato masher

wooden spoon

serving bowls

Sharp knives and boiling liquids are dangerous.

6. Remove the saucepan from the heat. Use a potato masher to make the mixture into a pulp.

7. Reheat the mixture in the saucepan over a low heat. Stir it gently with a wooden spoon so that it doesn't stick to the pan. Add water if the mixture is too thick for a soup. Then add salt to taste.

8. Wash the cilantro leaves and dry them. Then chop them finely.

9. Pour the soup into serving bowls and sprinkle cilantro over the top to decorate the soup.

Stuffed tacos

Tacos are simply tortillas folded in half to make a U-shape and then fried. They can be stuffed with many different sauces and fillings, hot or cold. They can be eaten as snacks or served at the start of a meal. You can buy taco shells and stuff them with fillings of your choice. Here are some suggestions:

Finely chopped red and green peppers and fresh tomato slices, mixed with avocado dip

Peeled shrimps or prawns, mixed with avocado dip

Slices or diced chunks of cold cooked turkey, mixed with cooked tomato sauce.

Ingredients

1 onion

1 sweet red pepper

1 cup fresh *or* canned tomatoes

1 tsp freshly chopped cilantro

1 green chili

1 T tomato puree

black pepper

salt

Cooked tomato sauce

You could serve this sauce with fried or grilled turkey breasts or roast duck, and boiled new potatoes.

1. Peel the onion. Using a sharp knife, carefully chop the onion and sweet red pepper very fine. Be sure to keep your fingers away from the knife blade.

2. Chop the tomatoes coarsely with a knife. If you are using fresh tomatoes, wash them and peel off the skins before you chop them up. If you are using canned tomatoes, drain the juice before you measure them.

Equipment

sharp knife

chopping board

colander

measuring cup

large saucepan

wooden spoon

large bowl

Ask an adult to help you when you start to cook.

Sharp knives and boiling liquids are dangerous.

3. Wash the cilantro leaves and dry them. Then chop them fine.
4. Wash the green chili and dry it.
5. Put the chopped onion, red pepper, tomatoes, cilantro, the whole chili, and the tomato puree into a saucepan.
6. Bring the mixture to a boil and then simmer over a low heat for 20 minutes or until it is thick. Stir it gently with a wooden spoon so that it doesn't stick to the pan.
7. Using the wooden spoon, take the green chili out of the saucepan. Add black pepper and salt to taste.
8. If you are not serving the sauce immediately, let it cool down in the saucepan. Then put it into a bowl and store it in the refrigerator until you are ready to use it.

Mexican hot chocolate

Ingredients
½ lb semisweet cooking chocolate
4 cups milk
¼ tsp ground cinnamon
2 drops vanilla

Ask an adult to help you when you start to cook.

1. Break the chocolate into small pieces. Put the pieces in the top of the double boiler *or* into the heatproof bowl.
2. Fill the bottom of the double boiler *or* a large saucepan with cold water. Then bring the water to a boil. Turn the heat down so that the water continues to boil gently.
3. Put the container with the chocolate over the one with the boiling water. With a wooden spoon, stir the chocolate until it has melted.
4. Measure out the milk and pour it into another saucepan. Heat the milk gently but do not let it boil. Pour the melted chocolate into the hot milk.
5. Add the cinnamon and the vanilla to the mixture and bring the mixture to a boil.
6. Turn the heat down and whisk the mixture for 2 minutes until it is foaming.
7. Pour the chocolate into mugs and use the small whisk to whisk the chocolate again, so that there is foam on the top of each mug.

Equipment
measuring cup
double boiler *or* large heatproof bowl and saucepan
wooden spoon
saucepan
large and small whisks
4 mugs *or* cups

Sharp knives and boiling liquids are dangerous.

GLOSSARY

altitude: The height at which something is situated, usually above sea level.

aqueduct: A bridge or channel built to carry water. The Aztecs used pipes made of clay to make aqueducts. Each aqueduct had two pipes, so that there was a constant supply of water even when one of the pipes was being cleaned.

astrologer: Someone who studies the effects that the movements of the stars and planets may have on people's actions and behavior on earth.

astronomy: The scientific study of the stars and planets and other objects in space.

bartering: Using goods to buy other goods, instead of using money. The Aztecs often used cacao beans to make up the difference between the price or value of the goods that they were bartering.

botanical: Describes the scientific study of plants. A botanical garden is a place where plants are collected and grown so that they can be studied.

causeway: A raised road or path over wet ground or water.

city-state: A small state or area of land, which is centered on a single city and governed by it.

colony: A group of people from one country or area who have settled in a different country or area, but who are ruled by the country that they came from. The place where the colonists settle is also called a colony. The land in the colony is claimed as part of, or belonging to, the country that rules the colony.

conquest: The victory of one country or people over another, usually through battles or wars. The Spanish not only defeated the Aztecs and took all their valuable goods, particularly their gold, but also took control of their lands and ruled the Aztec empire as a Spanish colony.

convert: To persuade people to change their beliefs and turn from one religion to another.

drought: An unusually long period without rain or snow.

elect: To choose one person from a group of people for a particular position or job.

empire: A group of countries or states, ruled by a single government or an emperor.

estate: An area of land, usually in the countryside, owned or controlled by one person.

famine: A time when there is not enough food to feed everyone, usually when the crops have failed, so people die of starvation.

fertile: Rich in the foods that help plants to grow well.

fertilize: To spread plant and animal waste on the land and then dig it into the land in order to enrich the soil. The Aztecs used mud and rotting plants from the lakes, and human and animal waste as fertilizers.

fiber: A threadlike substance, taken from plants or animals, mainly used by the Aztecs to weave cloth.

herb:	A plant used in cooking to add flavor to food or as a medicine.
inherit:	To have the right by law to receive goods, possessions, land, or money when their owner dies.
irrigate:	To bring water to crops. To do this, the Aztecs dug ditches and water channels, or canals, wide enough for boats to use.
legend:	An old story that many people believe, even though it may not be quite true.
merchants:	People who bought and sold goods, often from other countries. The Aztec merchants owned the canoes and paid for the porters, whom they organized to transport goods from one place to another. The *pochteca* also carried goods for the nobles and the *tlatloani*, and traded them abroad.
ocelot:	A large South American wildcat, similar to a leopard.
preserve:	To treat food or drink so that it could be kept for a long time without going bad. The main ways the Aztecs preserved food were by salting it or leaving it to dry in the sun. They may have smoked meat and fish to prevent them from going bad quickly in the heat. They probably used spices and vinegar to pickle vegetables to preserve them. Frozen and canned foods were unknown at that time
reservoir:	A large container, such as a tank or a lake, where water is collected and stored as a supply for a town or city.
revenue:	Money, produce, or goods that are an income from one or many sources.
scribe:	Someone whose job is to write things out by hand or to keep written records.
staple:	The most important or main food, crop, or goods produced in a particular area.
thatch:	To make a roof of dried straw or reeds.
tribute:	Regular payments in goods or money made by one state or area to another. The Aztecs threatened and sometimes went to war with the states or areas that refused to pay tribute to them or that did not keep up their regular payments to them.
tropical:	From the middle and hottest part of the world, between the lines made by the Tropic of Cancer to the north and the Tropic of Capricorn to the south.
wicker:	Twigs, often from a willow tree, that have been braided together. Wicker is often used to make baskets, seats, or fences.

Further reading

Berdon, Frances F. *The Aztecs*. New York: Chelsea House, 1989.

Dineen, Jacqueline. *The Aztecs*. New York: New Discovery Books, 1992.

Hicks, Peter. *The Aztecs*. New York: Thomson Learning, 1993.

Marrin, Albert. *Aztecs and Spaniards: Cortés and the Conquest of Mexico*. New York: Atheneum, 1986.

Odijk, Pamela. *The Aztecs*. Morristown, New Jersey: Silver Burdett Press, 1990.

Shepherd, Donna A. *The Aztecs*. New York: Franklin Watts, 1992.

INDEX